HAL•LEONARD
INSTRUMENTAL PLAY-ALONG

AUDIO ACCESS INCLUDED

TROMBONE
JAMES BOND

T0066183

PLAYBACK+
Speed • Pitch • Balance • Loop

To access audio visit:
www.halleonard.com/mylibrary

Enter Code
2486-2557-1073-2441

Audio arrangements by Peter Deneff

ISBN 978-1-4950-6084-7

Music Sales America

EXCLUSIVELY DISTRIBUTED BY

7777 W. BLUEMOUND RD. P.O. BOX 13819 MILWAUKEE, WI 53213

Visit Hal Leonard Online at
www.halleonard.com

TITLE	PAGE

DIAMONDS ARE FOREVER

from DIAMONDS ARE FOREVER

Words by DON BLACK
Music by JOHN BARRY

TROMBONE

FOR YOUR EYES ONLY

from FOR YOUR EYES ONLY

TROMBONE

Lyrics by MICHAEL LESSON
Music by BILL CONTI

FROM RUSSIA WITH LOVE

from FROM RUSSIA WITH LOVE

TROMBONE

Words and Music by
LIONEL BART

GOLDFINGER
from GOLDFINGER

TROMBONE

Music by JOHN BARRY
Lyrics by LESLIE BRICUSSE and ANTHONY NEWLEY

JAMES BOND THEME

TROMBONE

By MONTY NORMAN

8

LIVE AND LET DIE
from LIVE AND LET DIE

TROMBONE

Words and Music by PAUL McCARTNEY
and LINDA McCARTNEY

NOBODY DOES IT BETTER
from THE SPY WHO LOVED ME

Music by MARVIN HAMLISCH
Lyrics by CAROLE BAYER SAGER

TROMBONE

ON HER MAJESTY'S SECRET SERVICE - THEME

TROMBONE

By JOHN BARRY

SKYFALL

from the Motion Picture SKYFALL

TROMBONE

Words and Music by ADELE ADKINS
and PAUL EPWORTH

Slowly, with feeling

A VIEW TO A KILL

from A VIEW TO A KILL

TROMBONE

Words and Music by JOHN BARRY
and DURAN DURAN

WRITING'S ON THE WALL

from the film SPECTRE

TROMBONE

Words and Music by SAM SMITH
and JAMES NAPIER

YOU ONLY LIVE TWICE

from YOU ONLY LIVE TWICE

Music by JOHN BARRY
Lyrics by LESLIE BRICUSSE

TROMBONE